# REAL BIG AMERICAN ZEN

## BY BRANDON WHITE

Raw Earth Ink

2021

This book is a work of poetry.

First paperback edition May 2021

All photographs and digital art by Brandon White
Cover concept by Tilly McGill
Cover and interior design by tara caribou

ISBN 978-1-7360417-2-7 (paperback)

Published by Raw Earth Ink
PO Box 39332
Ninilchik, AK 99639
www.taracaribou.com

*For Kenzie and our little birds*

In
Search
of
a
Center

# I

The air outside is cool,
the sky clear
and the deepest of blues.
Birds fly overhead,
ants march in long lines.
Rivers flow and
tree limbs sway
in the breeze.

Just as it has always been
and yet entirely different,
as you yourself are changed
from one moment to the next.
The boy who couldn't stand
the idea of his hometown,
now a man who couldn't imagine
dying anywhere else.

I wonder when the bodies
will start piling up around here?
I wonder when we'll
bulldoze them into trenches
and set them to burning?
When we'll watch
the black smoke rise
into all that blue.

## II

I think when this is all over,
I'll take up gambling.
Hit all the casinos
along the Oklahoma border,
develop my own strategies,
and feel that indescribable rush
of really putting it all on the line.

Then again, I could easily end up
like Big John and his many hats:
walking up and down the avenue, lost,
duffel bag over his shoulder,
wearing cargo pants
with every pocket filled,
love nowhere to be found.

Who the hell am I kidding?
I could never do that
to my wife and kids.
Romantic ideas
often make for
a shit
reality.

## III

Five people
sleeping on concrete
outside the bus station.
Poverty is
a worsening issue in our area,
but the city is doing nothing
about it.

It's far worse in other places.
In Vegas, they've made a parking lot
a sort of homeless camp.
I saw photos of men and women
laying blankets over the pavement,
but nothing seems to soften the world.

What happens if the sickness
spreads among these people?
Will a ventilator be available if a doctor
has to decide between
an upstanding citizen and a bum?
Sometimes there are no second chances.

## IV

My daughter struggles
to fall asleep on her own,
so we bought a night-light
that projects a moon and stars
onto the ceiling.
Last night she asked me to
stay with her,

so I squeezed
my broad frame onto the little bed
and watched her eyes
grow heavy and eventually close.
I stayed a while after,
watching her chest rise, fall,
no sight more beautiful to God or man.

"I love you, little bird," I whisper
before rolling onto my back
and staring up
into the endless
swirling chaos
from which all our love
and pain
sprang forth.

Update:

there is
no
center.

## Soaking in an Inflatable Pool
## Bought on a Whim

It took me an hour
to fill this thing,
but it was worth it.
If anyone's looking for me,
tell them I'm
in an inflatable pool
on my back patio,
eyes closed,
with the sun in my face
and a beer in my hand.

My chain link kingdom.
The lawn unmown,
a cloudless sky,
and lungs.
Laughing children
and barking dogs.
A few peaceful
moments carved
from the flesh
of Mother America.

## A Rainy July Afternoon

The park is empty on a wet
summer afternoon in anywhere America.
I'm surprised at how sad it makes me
to see the unused playground equipment.

Writing to you now
is difficult
and I second-guess
every word.

Masked faces
and tired eyes,
the world has become
these tired eyes.

I've got 20 minutes
of lunch hour to burn;
the sound of rain
lulling me into a dreamless sleep.

# Father & Son

They're eating tamales
at the table across from me.

The father.
and son.

So many similarities,
the way they hold their forks,

their posture,
the inflection in their voices.

The son is engaged
in conversation with the father.

That's good.
He doesn't know

how I'd come across
this table,

if he were staring at
his goddamn phone.

One day he'll be willing
to lose a hand

to have this moment
back.

## Be Here Now

How are you today?
I hate asking.
I hate being asked.
I'm not sure that I've
ever answered that
question honestly.

I'm told this isn't strange.
I suppose not.
If you were looking
for sad-sack poetry
you've come
to the right place.

I wish I could write
something truly romantic,
instead of all this
poor pitiful me shit.
I'd write about how
we could feed

on nothing but the love
in each other's eyes.
How we shouldn't
move an inch.
How we could
starve in this moment.

Unless you'd rather
order pizza.
If so, I'm down.
I just don't
feel like
cooking.

## Stuck Inside of Walmart with the Quarantine Blues Again

The man spoke loudly
into his phone
as I put cans of soup into my cart.
He wanted others to hear.
Like all cowards,
He needed someone to agree:

*They say*
*It's the Chinese virus,*
*'cause the Chinese*
*made it in a lab*
*as a means of*
*population control.*

*All I know is,*
*you better be happy*
*it ain't no goddamn socialist*
*in the White House,*
*Christ almighty,*
*could you imagine?*

*I'll tell you one thing,*
*ain't no damn virus*
*gonna keep me from livin'!*
*Only God knows when*
*my time is comin' so*
*me and mine ain't changin' a thing...*

Oh, Mama,

    could this

        really
be

    the

        end?

## Donut Day

Crying children and coronavirus
and heartburn and decent enough football.
Living room filling with smoke,
steaks burning on the stove.
whiskey burning
all
the
way
down.
I don't have it in me.
I don't have it in me.
I don't have it in me.


Welcome to Walmart,
the all purpose cleaner aisle
is looking pretty fucking bare.
4 cans of sanitizing spray
tucked under my arm,
can't
be
too
careful.
Sorry, we're all out.
Sorry, we're all out.
Sorry, we're all out.

A walking mid-life crisis
smirks at me as I adjust
the load I'm carrying.
He looks how Bradley Cooper
would look if force-fed donuts for days
        and
        days
        on
        end
Krispy Kreme Coop.
Krispy Kreme Coop.
Krispy Kreme Coop.

I could go the rest of my life
and never set foot
in another big box retail store.
No more tweety bird t-shirts
and shorts two sizes too small
           crammed
           into
             ass crack
              canyons.
God, if you're listening, save me.
God, if you're listening, save me.
God, if you're listening, save me.

Bradley Cooper is on the cover
of a magazine by the self-checkout.
Seems like such a nice guy.

## Restless

People are getting restless.
No, it's more than that.
People are filling the streets
in protest,
pandemic be damned.

They are gathering
in large groups,
shoulder to shoulder,
some armed,
without masks.

40,000 of our fellow
citizens are dead
at the time these words were typed.
They're filling refrigerated
trailers with bodies.

Tears fall from the windows
of apartment buildings in Queens,
where thousands
weep for a farewell
they've been denied.

As for me?
I'm drinking beer and watching
a beautiful couple
win 1.4 million dollars
on my favorite game show

and wondering
if we'll have football this year;
tired of waiting
for the world
to change.

# The Kill

Anxiety
has sat its fat-ass
on my chest,
turning
every breath into
war.

Damn you
for doing this
to me.
Damn me
for letting
you.

The pain
I've caused
was unintentional
and inexcusable.
Please forgive
my naivety.

What guarantees
do we have
in this life but
loss
and
regret?

They find us all,
scurrying like field mice,
oblivious to the sound
of beating wings,
of talons
reaching.

# The Odds

*Yes sir, I understand,*
*but the state STRONGLY*
*recommends this test*
*if there's any concern*

The coffee's hot,
and this cloudless morning
has enough chill in the air
to keep me happy

My energy level
is nonexistent,
and this lends the world
a dream-like quality

The Bradford Pear
sways in the yard
beyond our fence
like a living van Gogh

*The black and yellow*
*around the eyes*
*suggests your sinuses*
*have been inflamed a while now*

I cough every third breath
Last night I woke
and my throat felt like
an open wound

When I spat in the sink
the pink saliva
that swirled down the drain
came as no surprise

The fever broke a while ago
I'm drenched in sweat
and searching for poetry
in this fucking mess

*Your left ear is bulging*
*with infection*
*Are you sure you've*
*had no discomfort?*

You're trying to talk
to me, and I'm trying
to be here,
but I'm failing

My phone screen fills
with statistics
I tick the numbers up by one
to make room for myself

I silently add
life insurance totals to myself
The chance of my demise is minimal,
but I have a way of defying the odds

*We're just calling*
*to let you know*
*that the results*
*were negative*

I watch our children
play with kinetic sand
and notice how the sunlight
seems to dance in their hair

I exhale

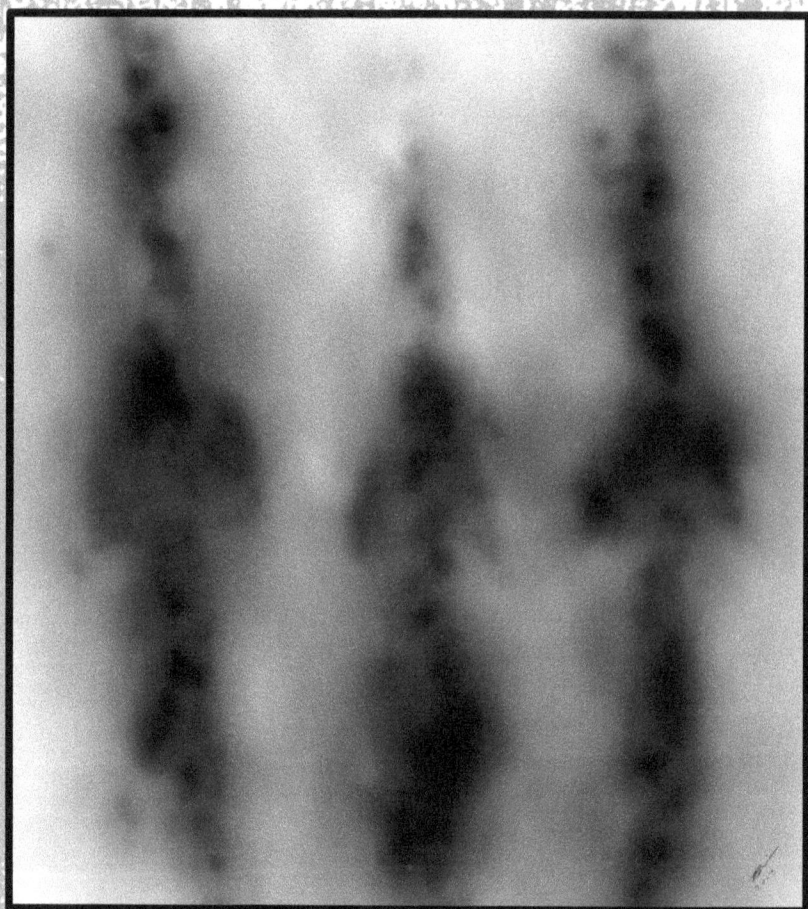

Dear Hank,

I admire your words until I don't. You knew the mystery by
name and you didn't tell a soul. You just sprinkled little
hints into the work, knowing the eyes that *could* see, *would* see
and the converted would guard the secret with their lives.

You wouldn't know what to make of the world I know, with
its equality and politically correct digital extermination squads
that would've hunted you down like a dog and sacrificed you
to the God of all you despised.

And a lot of the music sucks. Be glad you missed it.

Sincerely,


Brandon

## The Night Before

The screen on my phone
flashes every few seconds
as the well-wishes roll in.
It's 10:50 the night
before the day that caps off
the hardest year of my life,
and I can't even get to tomorrow
before it gets to me.

Everyone wants to be
first in line.

# Walking Down 9th Street in the Rain

The pavement beneath my feet
is wet and shiny.
The occasional drop of cold rain
on the back of my neck
is a shock to the system,
causing my jaw to clench.

I know plenty about cold,
rainy February days.
I know plenty about death.
I know I'm dreading the 27th
and at the same time, am ready.
I know I want to be free of it.

I know how a chest can rise and fall;
how what you think is the last breath
is really two irregular breaths before.
I know that I feel pulled to my childhood home
because I want to steal a rock
from the flowerbed.

I know that the people that bought this corner building
and made it their home
have these gas lanterns that burn all night
and I wonder what it must be like
to flush money.
I know my thoughts are all over the place.

I know I loved you.
I know I love you.
Not loved.
Love.

## From the Lobby of the Skirvin Hotel

Here on this couch
outside The Red Piano Lounge,
in the lobby
of the lovely
Skirvin Hotel,
I've lost count
of the drinks
and track of time.

They say this place is haunted;
that a woman jumped
from a tenth story window
not long after giving birth
to W. B. Skirvin's love child.
She had the baby in her arms
when she went through
the glass.

There will be no ghostly sightings
this evening, but the traditional
Scottish wedding taking place
on the thirteenth floor has brought
kilts aplenty to this evening's festivities,
and the man taking photos of
the chandelier from the second story balcony
is threatening to flash a bit of sack.

Wouldn't that be nuts? (Ba dum tss)

In all seriousness,
  I'm grateful to be here with you,
  drunk on good whiskey,
    knowing there's not a better
      conversation to be found in this city.
      Forget the world, spend the money,
        take my hand
          and melt    into    the night.

## New Car Smell

I remember the sun on my forearm
as we rode through town in your new car.
I remember the smell of the leather and
Van Halen blaring over the radio.

I remember you giving it the gas
as we merged onto the interstate,
my adrenaline surging, laughing nervously,
you easing on the breaks before the fear set in.

I'm lying awake tonight wondering
what became of that car?
There will never be a day
I don't miss you.

## The Dance

Roll out of bed
and into the dry mouth
of morning

Cold water splash
and a red-eyed
reflection

Cause and effect
and the wages
of sin

The night before
swirling down
the drain

A scalding baptism
burns everything
but a memory

We learn the dance
of death over
many years

A bottle presses
to lips like the barrel
of a gun

## Intentional Hair

A man addresses
a gathering of young professionals
from an unsteady podium
that has likely called this
conference room home
since the '70s.

He's noticeably uncomfortable,
keeping his back to most of the room
for the majority of his spiel.
His hair is longish,
he keeps a five o'clock shadow,
and has no noticeable accent.

The hair is intentional.
He's proud of it.
He keeps running his hand
through it.
VO5 Hot Oil Treatment,
Mane 'n Tail,

some of the weird stuff
made with essential oils
that you only get
through a subscription service.
I had long hair
once too.

His hand just ran through
his dark locks again
and I'm losing control.
My center vibrates with laughter,
but my face remains unchanged.

I don't feel well.
I'm being a dick.
I'm on the verge of
falling asleep.
VO5 Hot Oil Treatment.

A smile spreads
across my face.
A colleague leans over,
What's so funny?
Oh, it's nothing.

But the truth is,
It's everything,
and you
wouldn't get it,
Wonder Bread.

# Wellspring

Where has the wellspring gone?
Where are the words?
Where is my mind
if not attempting to drink in
the day and searching for
some trace of the sacred?

It's not in this half-eaten
plate of fajitas.
It's not in the glaring eyes
of the man I upset
by smiling
at his daughter.

It's not in my eyes, that
look back unblinking
until he thinks better
of the situation.
It's not in this car
listening to a book on Norwegian Black Metal.

It's not in the regret I feel
for staring back at the angry father,
or in the fact that I don't listen
to black metal at all,
I just find the whole thing
fascinating.

Or maybe it is?
Where else could it be found
if not in the passing
of every mundane
and extraordinary moment,
waiting to be recognized?

## Apologies to Mr. Ginsberg

Buzzing on rye,
eyes growing heavy
while reading Ginsberg's
greatest hit.

Sorry, Al.
It's not you.
I'm just all out
of fight.

Howl on.

## Gas Station Breakfast

The street-man and I make eye contact.
I look away.
I look back just as he does.
We lock eyes again.
He looks nervous,
following a well-dressed man
behind the convenience store.
He's gone to feed the beast
that gave him to the streets;
that keeps him here.
We are prisoners,
one and all.

It occurs to me
over gas station breakfast
that writing about hope
and joy bring neither
to my life.
I am neither hopeless
or without joy.
I ride a steady wave
of shoulder-shrugging
all right, I guess.
There are far worse
places to be.

Like on your knees
behind a convenience store,
having a whole
different kind
of gas station
breakfast.

## Cabin Fever

A poorly timed
rejection of any kind
is enough to send
flashes of epic violence

through the mind
of a working stiff.
One more thing
to remind him

of all the other things
that refuse
to fall
into place.

The child
that won't sleep,
the ignored text
turned unwanted call,

The unmasked
shoppers
that will surely
kill us all.

The old man breathing
down your neck
in the checkout
line.

There's no relief
to be had.
No amount of booze,
or jerking off,

or prayer,
or meditation,
or painting,
or reading,

my GOD don't
get me started
on these
poems!

The soul,
the soul,
the soul!
Your soul,

my soul,
his soul,
her soul!
Stirring in the soul,

bursting in the soul,
burning in the soul,
churning in the soul,
ENOUGH about the soul!

The word soul
is a lot like
the word
love;

Everyone uses it,
but very few know
what the hell they're
talking about.

Replace the word
soul
with the word
ass in your next work.

At least then
we can all
have a
laugh.

**Love Is**

I am not
an easy love.

I challenge
at every turn,

and I scoff
at convention.

I'm irritable
and a slave to the blues.

The depression,
my God, the depression.

I feel I owe you
a ten year apology

for every time you've
sat across the table

and stared into
lifeless eyes.

Forgive me,
love.

Forgive me
for every time

I didn't have
the strength.

Forgive me
for every hangover

that derailed
your momentum.

I promise
I'm trying.

And
I love you.

The smell
of your skin,

the taste
of your lips,

what would
I be without?

Heaven
is your hand in mine.

# Fingernails

My nails are a little too long.
I scratched
the back of my neck like a lover
as I slept
and it hurts
like hell.

I'm an adult now.
I work, raise children,
and drink
to forget the false dreams
of Mother America that die
with each passing day.

I saw my daughter's eyes
go wide at the sight
of snow this morning
and all I could think of
was the roads,
the ice, if I'd be late.

Christ, please my little loves,
cling to your wonder.
I'm not saying there's nothing
of worth on the other side of youth,
I'm saying it took many miles
and many tears to find it here with you.

There is love.
That much is true.
There is my love for you,
eternal and immutable.
All else remains subject
to change.

Dear Hank,

I made the mistake of joining a group of your followers in conversation about your work, hoping they might share some interesting thoughts on how they were changed by your words.

As it turns out, your acolytes have nothing interesting to say about your writing. As a matter of fact, they seem way more intrigued by the idea of you, than anything you put to paper.

They spout off little quips that are obvious attempts at occupying the void left. They've romanticized the idea of being a drunk, just as you did. Your art has very little to do with any of it. I found myself, again,
grateful that I hesitate before speaking. I sat back and watched as they made me love you a little less.

I wonder how long before they tire of the schtick and become someone else? Like I'm so different, right? We're all frauds in some way or another, just trying to find the skin that fits well enough that we forget to hate ourselves.

What does it mean to write a dead man anyway?

Stay Frosty,

Dubya

## Be

It's a wonderful life.

Though there's sickness,
and death,
and bodies melting
like candles
in trailers outside
the mortuary.

It's a wonderful life.

Though fear
and division threaten
the stability of our country,
and the house is rotting,
and I feel like a walking
panic attack,

It's a wonderful life.

The river rushes on.
The cardinal watches
through the window.
The mystery remains.
The Kingdom
is here.

## Wildfire Heart

Pull the t-shirt out of the dirty clothes
and iron it, those who saw

you wear it Monday
will have forgotten or assume

you washed it.
Finish your cup of coffee,

hell,
have another.

Let the hot shower
wash over you

without feeling
the need

to scrub,
wash hair,

and brush your teeth simultaneously.
Finish the chapter

while on the crapper.
Google your Father's

high school football
stats.

Be thankful
you were there

to say goodbye.
Be late.

Take the scenic route
and listen to beautiful music.

Stop for a breakfast
that sounds appealing

and don't settle
for the protein bar.

Finish the song
before killing

the engine.
Breathe in your existence.

Embrace a small act
of rebellion and

fan the flames
of your

wildfire
heart.

# Flow

I'm out of sync again,
out of the flow,
with nothing to give
that hasn't been given.

In my own way
is how I hope
each word,
each line

meets the page
and
where I continue
to find myself.

## Every Kiss

Every kiss
from your lips
tastes like
the possibilities
of a long
Friday night-

and I'm eighteen
again and full
of false bravado
and insecurities,
but confident
enough that

this irresistible
invitation that
draws my hands
forward will
see me
rise to the occasion

with unwavering
certainty.

## Big Blue Pickup

The man down the street
drove a big blue pickup truck.

He lived in a modest house.

He was blue-collar,
bred by blue-collar.

He had recently proposed
to his long-time girlfriend
and seemed happy.

He used to do yard work
for his friend of 35 years
who lived in the house
next to mine.

I'd see him,
shirtless and sweating
in the summer heat.

He was making plans
to love a woman
and build a life.

Last Thursday
he was being
especially affectionate
towards her before
she left to buy groceries.

He kept pulling her close
and kissing her deeply.

Laughing, she finally
broke away and left.

When she came home,
she found him hung
in their bedroom closet.

Three days later
the big blue pickup
is still in the driveway.

## God's Wrath
## in a Chevy Cruze

Little football-shaped pills
release the grip on my lungs
and I'm grateful when
the air comes easy.

Yesterday a bird flew
in front of my car
and was delivered
to its creator.

I've spent the better
part of two days
wondering if there was
more I could've done,

but I can't come up
with anything.
I was God's wrath
in a Chevy Cruze.

Beware all who
cross my path-
I am your reckoning,
and I get 32 miles

to the gallon.

### Regarding Flight

The sparrow sings her morning song
with no knowledge

of the heavy-hearted man
who listens below.

Would you fly if you were able?
I sure as hell wouldn't.

To see that far down the road
is not the ability to change where it leads.

So I'll keep my feet on the ground
and be grateful

that the things of the sky
return with songs of hope.

Together we watch the sun ascend
and set the horizon to burning.

## Regarding Tantric Yoga

Ankle-deep
in insecurities
and I fear I'm
on the brink
of losing the plot
completely.

I find myself
worrying that
my voice only
muddy's the water,
that plenty of others
say it better.

Every line that
finds the page
feels cliché,
worn out,
too precious
for its own good.

A couple of months ago
I didn't feel this way.
A couple of months ago
I didn't give a
fiddlers fuck for
anyone's opinion

except for the
handsome bastard
looking back at me
while brushing the stale
taste of whiskey from
his mouth each morning.

So what happened?
Well, when I figure that out
I'll stop drinking,
lose 40 pounds
and take up tantric yoga
so I too can fuck

for seven straight hours
like Sting.
In the meantime,
I fully intend
to roll onto my stomach
sometime today.

## Bob and Weave

A can of tuna,
a sleeve of crackers,
three drinks in
on a Sunday night-
there's not a man breathing
more content than I.

It's a beautiful thing,
getting out
of your own way.
I'd like to take this
time to remind myself
that I'm undefeated

against my asshole brain
with its constant comparisons,
envious thoughts
and obsessive nature.
To push through your
desire to self-destruct

is to parry the punch
and deliver
a strike of your own.

### Reassurance

Oh this,
the blessing
of little bodies
that beg to be held

of little hands
that reach
in the night
for reassurance

Oh this,
our legs
entwined beneath
blankets and stress

our heads
resting
on opposite ends
of the couch

Oh this,
the twitching of toes
says I'm needed,
and you don't know

how dark it gets
in this living room
when you go to bed early
and it's just me

and that little voice
that turns every
shadow into a
noose

## Sardines

Sardines
mean a great many things
to people.

For many, it's a crinkled nose
and a shaking head,
a protruding tongue.

For some, it's a paycheck
and their kid's shoes
for the new school year.

For others, it's a delicacy
of the highest order
and to be revered.

For me, it's something of an adventure,
having never tried them,
three cans and a box of saltines

tucked under my arm
like something precious
that must be saved.

I hurry to the self-checkout,
drunk on the first adrenaline
I've felt in three months.

May I be
forever ruled
by my curiosities.

## Shame

There's a muzak
speaker
above
the toilet
in the
employee
bathroom.

I hate to complain,
but this dump
deserves
a better
soundtrack
than The Killers
latest.

## Regarding Introductions

Introductions
have always been tricky
for me

be it conversation or poem,
I tend to fall
all over myself

in an attempt
to be both approachable
and friendly.

It almost always
comes across — and feels —
forced.

I like people
as much as my constitution
allows,

which is to say
I prefer the company
of my family, a few friends

and nearly
no one
else.

As far
as the poems
are concerned?

Don't think I won't
"Once upon a time"
this shit.

# I Was Hoping For Rain

No, No, No!
Don't    let    the    blue    sky    through!
With  its  empty  promises
and  oppressive  heat!

I woke to the rain
and felt my heart rise in me
for the first time in days,
but the blue on the horizon
keeps growing
along with my disappointment.

Arkansas  borders  Oklahoma,
Kansas,  Missouri,  Tennessee,
Mississippi,  Louisiana,  Texas
and      Hell,
but no map  will  tell  you  that.

To step outside on any   typical
summer's day is to
feel  the  Devil's  ass-crack
hanging
o
v
e
r
your
h e a d.

## The Stranger

A state of flux.
Chained to formula
and consideration
for what words one
might consider musical,
when the meaning of music
has undergone a radical
shift in my life.

These bad habits,
wedged and triggered
from somewhere
in the dark murk
of my subconscious,
do no favors
and usually derail
all hope of creativity.

But here
I am.
Pushing through.
Each word
that finds
the page
a battle
won.

Look closer,
you can see
how the blood
has mixed with
these words.
How something
of me becomes
something of you.

## Boiled

Sahara dust turns
the Arkansas sky
into a dreamy haze, but does
nothing for the heat.
Sahara dust.
2020's been a weird one.

This morning my coffee mug's
handle snapped off
as I lifted it to drink;
It took a chunk of skin
from my index knuckle
and set my balls on fire.

So here I stand,
staring out at the milky sky,
my hand under a cold tap,
nuts boiled.

## Solitary Thoughts

Built like a brute
with a songbird heart
that breaks
with alarming
regularity,
I often question
my durability
in a life
like this.
But I've proven
to myself and others
that these broad shoulders
we're built for carrying
whatever needs carrying,
including the weight of the world.

But that isn't what any
of this has been about.
Blah blah blah,
I'm so different,
blah blah blah,
no one understands me.
The garage door lifts slowly,
and my eyes are drawn
to a small wasp's nest
that's got my trypophobia
all kinds of fucked up.
I walk into the house,
see the small wooden box
that contains my father
and wonder why I do this to myself.

I sit in the silence
of this empty house,
ground zero of my
greatest hurt,
when I could've had lunch
in my car.

I've got a lot of bad habits
and terrible self control.
I won't give up
until my heart gives in.
That seems to be the modus operandi.
Change is needed.
Change is welcome.
Change is coming.
Right?

# Nothing Darker

You,
the savior of reason,
the one who found
the hidden thread
that unravels the mystery
and sends God tumbling
from his throne
to the rocky earth below.

You,
stranger to empathy
and guardian
of the propaganda
machine,
who fights biases
with biases and
idealism with idealism.

You,
who's cock and gun
are one and the same,
a semi-automatic
mental masturbator,
who strikes at hope
with all the fury in
your nationalist heart.

You,
take this razor to
that mustache, but
please nothing darker,
as you are her lighthouse,
and that makes you
more than a
blood-bag.

You,
who steals my precious
minutes and fills
my mind and mouth
with venomous words
and thoughts
that bring about
overwhelming shame.

You,
my accidental teacher,
my walking reminder,
my tin soldier,
my thief,
you too can
be saved.

Dear Hank,

I can't seem to stop thinking about Tony, strung up and blue. I see him now in 65-inch high definition immortality and wonder what sent him over the edge? I've read countless articles that blamed everything from his drinking, to an unfaithful lover, to conspiracies that he was set to reveal a sex-trafficking ring. No one fucking knows.

What does it mean for the rest of us when a man of such enviable privilege, whose entire life sparked with adventure, decides to check-out early?

I guess that's the magic of television.

Be good or be good at it,


B-Dubya

## Lost Boy

He never stops pedaling
that worn-out bicycle.
From Garrison Avenue,
to the streets of Sallisaw,

he pedals at a furious pace
to escape the hell
that follows him.
The hell of his mind,

his broken mind,
his fried-egg mind,
his pre-destined mind,
his flawed genetics,

his flawed decisions,
his flawed appetites,
the flawed love
of his flawed mother

and the mother
that came before.
Does God answer
those who scream in the night?

Who fill Sallisaw streets
with banshee wails?
Does God answer
the ghosts of Garrison Avenue?

The lost children
of lost children?
What becomes of
the lost children?

They pedal
all through the night.

# Regarding Lunchtime Meditation

Each day I perform a picture-perfect
Olympian-esque dive into the dark
pool of my subconscious.

That murky depth from which
sprang the first flickers of human thought,
imagination, your mother's voice,

your father's hands,
the soft breast of your first love,
the smell of coffee,

every damn book, song,
painting, sculpture,
Manhattan,

the first tongue you felt
other than your own,
every feeling of love

or suicidal urge,
war and it's many instruments,
every killer and perversion,

every Holy word in every
Holy scripture,
every body that would

enter another body
in search of the elusive whole,
all is found

here.

# The Lesson

My children, you are the only hope
I hold for this country, this world.
My open-hearted, wide-eyed
little birds.
You must find a way
to love the world,
even at its most
undeserving.

You see, suffering is the river
from which we drink.
Suffering is our great teacher.
Suffering is the lesson,
the gateway.
To know true love
is to know
true suffering.

Joy waits through
the doorway of suffering.
Step through it
without trepidation
and be enlightened.
There is nothing
to fear, little birds.
Love is the raft

that carries us
downstream
and beyond.

## To a True Artist

This morning I saw a man
sitting outside a café downtown
wearing an open Tommy Bahama shirt,
shorts and loafers.

He was bald and had a mustache
that was curled at the ends.

He sat smoking a cigarette and
plucking the strings of a violin,
occasionally stopping to sip his coffee.

The man sat in front of his car,
an old red Ford Explorer
with the word ART in big, bold letters
on the back windshield
and the driver's side door.

He'd positioned himself on a lawn chair,
unusually close to the road.

It all seemed so intentional;
the outfit, the mustache,
the need to pluck violin strings
within inches of busy morning traffic.

I miss smoking, only all the time, though.

This guy, his confidence, his smokes,
his music- the fucker.

The light turned green
and I swore I wouldn't
give him the attention
he so obviously craved—


and then I sat at my desk
and wrote a poem for the artist,
and his art-mobile,
and his addictions,
and his violin,

and knew that I am
every bit as full of shit.

## Ouroboros

I left a trail of tears
in a figure-eight pattern
as I moved about the kitchen.

Figure-eight.
Ouroboros.
Grief eternal.

I found you today
in the smell
of a drawer,

and tonight I'll lose you
again in a glass
of beer.

Figure-eight.
Ouroboros.
Grief eternal.

## Killer

You sound like a song
at the end of the world,
like the thoughts
of a killer.

I sway
here alone
to the melody
of your madness.

## Witness

Understand,
as I place this gentle kiss
upon your neck,
that I'll be requiring
every inch of you.

I've no desire to own
or tame, I simply wish
to experience you in your entirety.
To bear witness
to something truly
magnificent.

You are
the healing hands
of Christ.

You are
my redeemer.

Down on my knees
in the dark,

I'm a true
believer.

# Junkie Child

When she walked into the gas station,
I wasn't sure what I was seeing.
Orange hair, white button-up shirt,
jeans too long for her legs
but long enough to pad her
shoeless feet,
hunched over in some
otherworldly angle.

She placed a large can of beer
by the register
and laughed maniacally
at a joke only she knew.
She turned to me and
pulled down her mask,
revealing her sore-covered face
and brown teeth.

I stared into those hopeless eyes.
The eyes of the damned.
Filthy, drugged out of her mind-
barring some miracle,
all that's left is the dying.
Someone held her as a child,
or maybe they didn't.
Someone should've.

She smiles
like a
sunset.

## Peppers

Little green eyes meet mine

and a smile spreads across

my daughters face.

I can see that something

important is on her mind.

Daddy?

Yes, love?

I don't like peppers.

Neither do I.

Not entirely true,

but I won't ruin

this perfect moment

by being anything

other than

agreeable.

## Catalog

To walk into the room
and find the child's face
smeared with lipstick,
holding an open bottle of pills.

I instantly picture her small limp
body in my arms.
Me, mouth open,
screaming in the face

of all the tomorrow's
I refused to face
without
her.

This morning
she smiles over
a small green bowl
of cereal.

I smile back,
with a heart so light
the wind might just
carry it off.

## Weaponized
## Silence

Close enough
to smell your shampoo,
and lonelier
than
ever.

## Writers Block
## is Blocking
## the Writer

Inside
my head

rusty
gears turn

their
vibrations

make
my teeth

grind
and head

pound
and nothing

finds
the page

but
frustration

## Autopilot Promises

Men are clearing the streets
of debris from last night's storm
and I'm stuck in traffic
not feeling a thing.

This is the grind
they warn you about
when you're a kid;
the soul crusher.

I've given a lot of thought
to the small parts of us
that die unnoticed
in our pursuit of security,

like little suicides.
Pieces fall away,
but the body keeps
working.

Muscle memory
and bad habits
and a mind on autopilot
makes no promises,

so nothing new
is broken.

## Good Intentions

I could throw my
rage into the world,
and perhaps
the flames would
jump a bit higher
at my doing so,
but nothing
new would
be revealed.

Dead eyes
will still clog
the interstates
and traffic stops
and restaurant booths.
Dead love
will still hang heavy
in the space between
husbands and wives.

Dead dreams
will haunt the company
men and women
that spin the wheels
of our dying America,
and I'll be no closer
to feeling better
about how we
left things.

## Irish Dreams

We'll leave tonight
to the Dublin of my mind

where we'll drain pints
and whiskey neat

and in the morning
we'll burn in our hangovers

and I'll greet your
waking eyes with tea

and you'll love
a broken man

for the sincerity
in his effort.

Dear Hank,

I'm pretty sure JT was back on the junk, so I can't say I'm completely shocked to hear he's gone. Look at me, assuming, like so many of the shit-touchers polluting the interwebs.

A son has died, a father, a friend, a husband, and I'm assuming.

I'm still waiting to hear what exactly happened. Maybe sometimes the heart just up and quits. That sounds like something he'd say, doesn't it?

Pour a strong one tonight for a true man of melody.


Pour one for me too,


BW

### Acceptance

Loving you
is going to kill me,
and I'd have it
no other way.

And you tell me
I never say
anything
romantic.

# I've Found
# These Things
# to be True

A drunk,
with his swollen eyes,
pounding head,
parched throat,
and all his regrets,
can learn to love
the morning.

A daughter,
with her anxiety,
her trauma,
her warped
world view,
can never fully forgive
the absent father.

A bullet,
in a second,
will know
a person better
more intimately
than they ever
knew themselves.

Your heroes,
will kill themselves
in droves
and shatter
what faith
you have left
in the world.

                Your children,
                will ask
                for chocolate milk,
                and you'll recognize,
                briefly,
                the face
                of God.

Your fingers,
will graze
the ingrown hair
on your cheek
at the wrong moment,
and you'll picture a
soft throat and teeth.

                My hatred,
                is as pure
                as my love,
                as absolute,
                and I reserve it
                for but a special
                few.

## Regarding the Anger
## I Keep Hid

There was no perfect way
to do for you
what had to be done.

All I wanted
was for you to die
with dignity,

but I knew and know
that my reassurances
likely rang hollow.

However,
you knew you
were loved.

I suppose
there's comfort
in that.

I glimpse
happiness
on occasion,

and work
to be a worthy
father.

I
no longer
fear death,

and God
remains
unforgiven.

Somewhere
in the world
as I type this,

a child dies
in their mothers
arms.

Somewhere
in America
as I type this,

a mother dies
alone in a
hospital room,

her children
cry out to her
from an iPad screen.

I suppose
God has much
to answer for.

I'm not sure
anything more obvious
can be said.

## William Bronk
## is a Sad Ghost

William Bronk's voice
speaks to me
through Bluetooth.

Technology
has raised
the dead.

From the
little black box
by the bathroom sink,

through the hiss
and crackle
of time,

he bemoans
a world,
a life.

I spend much
of my time
among the dead.

# No
# Immediate
# Family Members
# Survive

The final line
in a local obituary
for a quiet
older man:

No immediate
family
members
survive.

A library
has burned.
A world
has vanished,

and there was
no one
left to
notice.

## Mercy Kill

Shake your head
and bite your tongue
at the memory
of saying some
truly dumb shit.

No one lives
without dragging
a few embarrassing
yesterday's
along.

Your forgiveness
feels like a lie,
and I don't have
the courage to
say I hate your love.

It hits me like
the hallmark channel,
all your horrible
acting.
Show mercy.

## Hunter/Hunted

My depression is wet
at the corners of its mouth,
heaving in the corner
of my bedroom, wild-eyed
and salivating at the idea of
me walking into the same old trap.

Through swollen sinuses
and head-splitting pressure
I raise a middle finger
and blow
raspberries
to my forever foe.

## Bedlam

Muffled voices fall from
the vent in the ceiling
and land like cannonballs
in my little sea
of tranquility.

A smile spreads
across my face,
thinking of
all the wild love
that waits

to rush into
my open arms.

## Fool

A shift occurs
as you settle into life

a gradual dying of
the fight inside a person

burying the dream in the backyard
while the neighbors sleep

God grabs his bags and
sneaks away in the night

leaving you on the couch
entranced by Robert Downey Jr

covered in Cheeto dust
and remembering sixteen

A door opens down the hall
and shuffling footsteps approach

A heavy-eyed child crawls
into your lap and returns to dreaming

The lucky ones find
new reasons to fight

The lucky ones find
new dreams

I've never considered
myself lucky

and for this
I'm a fool

## Cold

Call me crazy, but I don't mind
a nasty cold at the birth of Fall

The swimming head and eyes,
the aching body blanket wrapped

The swollen sinuses blowing
bright green heat

The inflamed airway,
lungs turned inside out

drifting in and out of sleep
to the sound of effervescent tablets

The minor suffering
turns my vices into strange dreams

I cough until my chest
rings hollow as Sunday faith

then dream a dream
where I never take you for granted

## She Colors the World

She's the kind of woman
that makes a man
want to change
his ways.

He won't,
but she sure makes
him believe
he could.

She breathes
possibility
into the
perfumed air.

She
colors
the
world.

## Clarity

No one ever told me
that the most beautiful sound
I'd ever hear
would be that of two off-key
little voices lifted in song.

No one ever told me
that this sound had the power
to dispel any darkness
of mind
or spirit.

Little fingers
trace my palm,
studying knuckles and scars
like the map of
some strange world.

All the riches of heaven
pale in comparison
to the love
I've
known.

## Lungs

What are your
clear, expanding lungs,
if not loving reminders
that today contains
all the potential
you need
to change
everything

## To My Friend, Wherever You Are

I remember running down Grinnell Avenue,
back to your house
with a stolen pack of cheap cigarettes
in your pocket
from the corner gas station.

You tore off the foil
and our mouths watered
at the sight of 20 class-A smokes
we were sure would
last for days.

When you got your Mustang,
we drove all night listening to Slayer,
smoking and talking about
the beautiful women
that stole our dreams.

You got suspended towards
the end of senior year
by that bastard Vice-Principal.
I skipped prom, and we
drank vodka long into the night.

You told me through clenched teeth
how you hated your Dad for leaving.
I knew you for twelve years before
he made an effort
to see you.

Your Mom died on Furman Street,
and I did my disappearing act
while you drank in the dark.
You'd call me crying
at 3 AM.

You never forgave me
for letting you face
that alone,
nor have I forgiven
myself.

I always think of you
after a few;
how there was
no other way
than this.

## Bohemian Dream

Windows
down

autumn wind rushing
through my fingers

Thinking of how I see you
now for what you are

My bohemian dream
my trick of the brain

You almost
had me fooled

## Real Big Zen

I'm locking this moment away, little bird.
There will come a time that you'll
require less of me, and this is all
I'll have left to hold.
This precious hour in
the shadow of a great maple,
an ancient observer,
you lay against my chest
as we slowly swing.

                    My Fathers spirit dancing in
                        the branches above us;
                    I prayed to recognize
                    this moment, little bird,
                    to appreciate its arrival.
                    To glimpse an existence
                        unencumbered by
                        the knowledge
                    of our impermanence.

I'm locking this moment away, little bird.
I'm locking it
into place where
I can always find you,
in the shadow of the great maple,
waiting to remind me
that love transcends
the demise of these earthly bodies
and dances in the trees,

                    waiting for us to remember
                    that we too have cause to dance.

## *Appendix*

"Junkie Child" first appeared in the Fall 2020 Anthology from Train River Publishing

"Clarity and Wildfire Heart" first appeared in the *Soon, A New Day* anthology from Quillkeepers Press

"Real Big Zen" and "Regarding Flight" first appeared in the *Creation and the Cosmos* anthology from Raw Earth Ink

**THE YEAR THAT STOLE THE LIGHT AWAY**

**BRANDON WHITE**

The Year that Stole the Light Away, the debut book of poems by Brandon White, is a remarkable journey through the depths of grief, heartbreak, and the first awkward footfalls back to a life rendered unrecognizable, yet budding with hope.

White guides us through a shared inevitability, offering a hand that we might navigate the darkness together and find our way back to something that resembles home.

Available online at Barnes and Noble, Amazon, and lulu. Signed copies available directly at brandonwhitemusicandpoetry.com.

## About the Author

Brandon White is a poet and songwriter from Fort Smith, Arkansas. His work has been featured in several anthologies and his debut collection of poetry, *The Year that Stole the Light Away*, was released in May 2020 from Raw Earth Ink.

White is also an accomplished songwriter, releasing several albums, EP's, and singles since 2007, with over 50 licensing deals for use of his work in retail environments and restaurants around the world.

White resides in Arkansas with his wife and twin daughters and is currently working on his third collection of poetry, *Take This Love and Build a Boat for the Sinking*.

www.ingramcontent.com/pod-product-compliance
Lightning Source LLC
LaVergne TN
LVHW011405080426
835511LV00005B/414